Blessed BY GOD

Broken BY LIFE

LEGAL DISCLAIMER

Blessed by God, Broken by Life
Copyright © 2022 Garcia Hanson-Francis.
All rights reserved worldwide.

No part of this material may be used, reproduced, distributed or transmitted in any form and by any means whatsoever, including without limitation photocopying, recording or other electronic or mechanical methods or by any information storage and retrieval system, without the prior written permission from the author, except for brief excerpts in a review. This book is intended to provide general information only. Neither the author nor publisher provides any legal or other professional advice. If you need professional advice, you should seek advice from the appropriate licensed professional. This book does not provide complete information on the subject matter covered. This book is not intended to address specific requirements, either for an individual or an organization. This book is intended to be used only as a general guide, and not as a sole source of information on the subject matter. While the author has undertaken diligent efforts to ensure accuracy, there is no guarantee of accuracy or of no errors, omissions or typographical errors. Any slights of people or organizations are unintentional. The author and publisher shall have no liability or responsibility to any person or entity and hereby disclaim all liability, including without limitation, liability for consequential damages regarding any claim, loss or damage that may be incurred, or alleged to have been incurred, directly or indirectly, arising out of the information provided in this book.

Connect with Magnetic Entrepreneur Inc.™
https://www.facebook.com/magneticentrepreneur
www.linkedin.com/in/magneticentrepreneur
E-Mail: magneticpublishing2017.com
Website: www.magnetic-entrepreneur.com

The following reflects my own recollections, experiences, and opinions and may not reflect the recollections, experiences, or opinions of the other people involved. Every statement herein is meant to be understood as my feeling, thought, assumption, joy, or frustration. No statements herein are meant as accusations or should be taken as irrefutable facts.

Book design by Olivier Darbonville

Blessed BY GOD
Broken BY LIFE

A SPIRITUAL BIOGRAPHY

Garcia Hanson-Francis

CEO, CADJPro Payroll Solutions

Dedication

I dedicate this book to the author and finisher of my faith, Jesus Christ.

Secondly, I dedicate this to my grandfather, District Officer Gayle and my higgler grandmother, Irene Sharpe for teaching me about motherhood and the power of prayer to achieve goals.

Lastly, I dedicate this book to the women who have the feeling that fear has paralyzed their lives. Live your purpose for the glory of God. To men, don't crowd the spotlight when your queen wants to shine; join in prayer and support her with the love that Christ instilled in you.

By Grace, through Faith, you never fail.

For your glory, Lord, I can do anything.

God will always be there for you every step of the way, so don't be afraid to pursue your dreams and do what you think is best.

The steps of a good man are ordered by the LORD: and he delighted in his way. Though he fall, he shall not be utterly cast down: for the LORD upholdeth him with his hand.

Psalm 37: 23-24

Contents

Acknowledgments IX
Foreword XIII
Prayer XV
Introduction XVII

Chapter 1 - Cousins..1
Chapter 2 - Canada.. 5
Chapter 3 - College 11
Chapter 4 - Payroll.. 15
Chapter 5 - Fired 19
Chapter 6 - Deondre...23
Chapter 7 - Aneurysm 27
Chapter 8 - Family 29
Chapter 9 - In-Laws 33
Chapter 10 - Baptism 37
Chapter 11 - Two... 41
Chapter 12 - Marriage 47
Chapter 13 - Health 53
Chapter 14 - Business...55
Chapter 15 - Twins..59
Chapter 16 - Secrets 67

Chapter 17 – Melane 71
Chapter 18 – Forgiveness 75
Chapter 19 – Future 79

Garcia Hanson-Francis 83
Testimonials 85
Conclusion 95

Acknowledgements

A Special Thanks to ...

The Most High God, my best friend and finisher throughout my life.

My four boys, who have inspired me to push forward to create a legacy for them. Thank you for being patient with me.

Pastor Lance Brown of Refuge City Pentecostal Church. Thank you for accepting me. And thank you to Team CPS, Gayle, Hanson and Wilson's Family.

My coach, Melane. Every day, I wish I'd met you sooner. You took me out of park and put me in drive. I will never forget our time together.

Robert J Moore. Thank you for bringing the ideas out and for believing that nothing is impossible. God is real!

The person who is able to listen to me and capture my story on paper. Faith, I am thankful for you and the journey ahead for us.

My friends, family, and fans that have supported me. You will always be a part of me.

And finally, my husband. Your egotistical ways pushed me so far and ultimately brought me closer to God. I've found my purpose by fighting through life's problems instead of running away. My fear is cancelled. My passion is thriving. I thank you.

Rejoice always, pray continually, give thanks in all circumstances; for this is God's will for you in Christ Jesus.

Hebrews 12:28-29

Foreword

I am honoured to write this Foreword for Garcia Hanson-Francis. It is very refreshing and rare to see a businesswoman who is totally sold out to the Lord, and who gives the Lord Jesus Christ top priority in her life and decisions.

It is no surprise that she has been recognized for her leadership skills by Inc. Magazine, RBC Women of Influence, Women Leaders Magazine, Excelligent Magazine and ByBlacks Peoples Choice.

She has influenced all those she has come in contact with, providing an example to be emulated for her work ethic, compassion, business knowledge and entrepreneurial success.

In addition to her Payroll expertise and CPM designation, she provides the skills for her husband's business, doing payroll and HR.

Even with the high level of accomplishment she enjoys, she will be the first to tell you that it has not come easily, but with many challenges, hardships, tears, frustration, fatigue and problems in her personal and family life.

Through everything, she has not wavered and leans on the Lord to work things out. Her example of depending on the Lord has been a wonderful testimony to her family, especially to her four boys. With the Lord's guidance and help, she is raising them to be men of God.

May the Lord help you, Garcia, as you continue your journey, and grant you much more success.

Robert J. Moore,
5X Bestselling Author and Publisher
Forbes Coaches Council
Guinness World Record Holder

Prayer

> "The Lord is near to all who call on him, to all who call on him in truth. He fulfills the desire of those who fear him; he also hears their cry and saves them."
>
> PSALM 145: 18-19

Dear God,

It's me again.

Thank you for all the things you've taught me. I understand your decisions. I accept my own decisions, good and bad, and I take responsibility for my free will. I ignored the signs and the intuition you gave me. I regret that I didn't trust in your love for me. I regret all the time I wasted being unhappy.

Father, I was tired of being tired. I wanted to be the person you designed. Thank you for helping me find the path where my service to you will be fulfilled.

I give myself to you completely, in awe of your magnificence. I trust that you are my Creator, who knows me better than I know myself.

I surrender myself to you and pray your light of love and hope will burn bright in me. Your love has never left me, and I know that now. You are my God, and without you, I am nothing. Thank you for giving me the strength to get where I am today. Thank you for the privilege of being a mother.

Please forgive me for not trusting in your plan all along. I accept the challenges ahead with gratitude, and I will trust in you.

In Your Name,

Amen

Introduction

> *"You have heard that it was said, 'Eye for an eye and tooth for a tooth.' But I tell you, do not resist an evil person. If anyone slaps you on the right cheek, turn to them the other cheek also."*
>
> MATTHEW 5:38-39

My name is Garcia Hanson-Francis.

My story starts in Jamaica. Had I stayed, this would be a much different story - perhaps shorter, perhaps lighter. But that wasn't the plan God had for me. As I continue to discover today, his plans for me were much bigger than that. God had trials and challenges - and opportunities to overcome - laid out before me from my birthplace to the distant horizon.

He drew me away from my mother's house to Canada to live with my father and, eventually, my husband. My obstacles multiplied by the day. I didn't know how to rid myself of the anger, frustration, and sadness, but I knew everything God needed me to know to get where He wanted me to be.

And so do you.

This is not a story about how hard my life has been. This isn't the sad diary of a poor, put-upon woman. This is a story of resilience, determination, forgiveness, and God.

God had a purpose for me - decided before I was even a twinkle in my father's eye - and it called me relentlessly. Even in moments of peace and good health, my soul was unsettled because I knew I wasn't where I was destined to go.

As you follow me north to Canada and on through school, marriage, motherhood, illness, and purpose, I hope you're smiling with me. Because even when things were at their worst, I was on a path that brought me closer to God and to spiritual fulfillment every day.

As you walk your path, remember God won't force you to follow Him. It takes faith and a burning desire to succeed - whatever success means to you. It takes courage and resolve. Sometimes you have to be willing to take the most difficult road. But if you show up for God, He'll show up for you.

CHAPTER 1

Cousins

"Do not fear, for I am with you; Do not be dismayed, for I am your God."

Isaiah 41:10

I grew up in the 80s in a typical Jamaican home. At least, it seemed to me like any other. My mother worked hard selling produce at the market four days a week. It wasn't much, but she managed to support me, my older brother, my two younger brothers, her parents, and a few cousins.

My father was usually gone. He lived in Canada, where he owned a small supermarket and was a seasonal farm worker. In Jamaica, he drove an ice cream truck and would always bring home ice cream for me when he was there.

We'd go for long walks in the evenings, sometimes two or three hours. We'd find a nice place to sit down.

I'd eat my ice cream while he told me stories about my

cousins and me, how we used to play together when I was too young to remember.

Later, I discovered that my "cousins" were my half-siblings. My father - my sweet and caring father - had been living a double life longer than I'd been alive.

He had a wife in Jamaica - a wife who wasn't my mother - and they had children. He had two families, but he seemed to love all of us the way a father should.

There were no misunderstandings between my mother and my father's wife. She was a patient and loyal woman who never treated my siblings and me any differently than her own children.

She became a second mother to me, and I was grateful for her. As a wife and mother, I can now imagine the emotional turmoil my father put her through. She was his wife, and he stepped out of their marriage to take another woman and start another family. And yet, she cared for him until he died of lung cancer in the autumn of 2006.

As the eldest daughter in my Jamaican household, most of the domestic responsibilities fell on me. I washed and dried and put away the laundry.

I managed everyone's medications. I gave baths and prepared meals, and checked homework. All of that, on top of taking care of myself. I took pride in my work and maintained high grades.

I went to church as often as I could throughout the week. I loved church. We had Bible study, choir, and many other activities that kept me busy.

I believed in God's message and felt content in His house. It was my place of solitude, where I stole a bit of peace from my full and busy life.

One Sunday afternoon, I came home from church to find out I'd made the honour roll at school. It was an award worthy of celebration. I was outside with my cousins - laughing, dancing, and having a great time - when I suddenly became dizzy and needed to lie down.

Something was wrong. My face felt frozen. I couldn't cry or call out. I couldn't tell my cousins to get help. I felt like I was falling.

To my relief, I heard one of my cousins say, "Run and get Grandma! Garcia is sweating. She looks like she's going to die. Don't worry; God wouldn't be so cruel. He'll save her. Go!"

Soon, my mother was at my side. I've never felt prayer so powerful before or since. My grandmother also prayed. She cried out to God until her gown was soaked in tears.

At the time, I didn't understand the power of prayer -

the power of God – but it saved my life that night. I spent the night cradled in my grandmother's arms.

When I awoke, I looked at myself in the mirror. My face looked normal. I felt fine. My cousins cried and told me how they'd thought I was pulling a prank on them and how scared they were.

They hugged me tight and told me how happy they were to see me back in full spirit.

I felt a distinct sense of warmth all around me. I remember thinking it was God's hug. He wanted me alive to continue my hard work.

The incident left me scared and confused, but I was reassured knowing that God was with me. If He wanted me here, nothing could pull me away. And I knew there was a voice and a meaningful purpose God was saving for me.

CHAPTER 2

Canada

"Do not mistreat or oppress the foreigner, for you were foreigners in Egypt."

Exodus 22:21

In 1997, when I was 15 years old, we were still using "snail mail." It took days for letters to reach my father in Canada. He didn't like waiting to find out how I was doing and not knowing what was happening in real time.

So he decided I would go live with him and his other children in Meaford, Ontario. It was a jarring change, but I got to live with my half-sister, who was born just three months before me, plus a brother, an older sister, and a younger sister my dad fathered with a white woman in Canada.

Meaford had maybe two other black people besides my family. It was an all-white town, but I still felt safe.

My siblings and I agreed that the white area was fine as long as we kept our heads down and focused on each other.

We always knew we had to look out for one another.

We spent all our time together and enjoyed a sense of community when the seasonal farm workers came to town. In Jamaican culture, Sunday dinner is the most important meal of the week, so my family cooked for the farm workers on Sundays. We shared our table, and it reminded me of home. I cherished it.

Just as I had back in Jamaica, I studied hard and got good grades, which led to scholarships and awards. I wasn't allowed a boyfriend, so I had no distractions from my studies.

Children at my school weren't used to the privilege of a diverse classroom, so despite my friendly demeanour, I endured a lot of bullying in school. When you're different, you're an easy target for children thirsting for a sense of power, control, and superiority. Kids tormented me with racial slurs and comments.

I prayed for the strength to let it roll off my back, and it worked. Without my attention, the bullies grew bored, and I surprisingly became quite popular with the other kids.

So, they targeted my sister instead. Annmarie was a talented artist, but she struggled in math. The schoolyard bullies used that to insult and terrorize her.

Eventually, we devised a plan to eliminate our weaknesses and shut them up. We made an arrangement. Annmarie would do my art assignments, and I'd do her math assignments. I couldn't draw a stick figure to save my life, so it was a win-win. We had excellent report cards that year, but bullies don't like to lose.

In Jamaica, we have a traditional drink called Sorrel Drink. It's a spiced hibiscus punch with the distinct holiday flavour of ginger and cinnamon. It's customarily served for celebrations, similar to eggnog.

Like eggnog, it's usually spiked with a touch of alcohol. For my 16th birthday, my sister and I brought Sorrel Drink to school. Our drink had a splash of rum and some red wine to deepen the flavour. Hindsight is 20/20, but it seemed harmless at the time.

One of the bullies asked if they could taste it. It had been a while since they'd thrown any sharp verbal jabs at us, and again, I was a friendly child, so we didn't think anything of it. That is until we heard, "Will Annmarie and Garcia please report to the office right away," over the school's PA system.

When we reached the office, we were greeted by police officers waiting to escort us home for having alcohol on school property. We tried to explain that it was a Caribbean tradition and that we weren't drinking at school, but no one listened to us.

We knew our dad would be waiting at home with a belt. He had received a call from the office staff telling him we had alcohol at school, so he must have thought we bought our own liquor somehow.

He wouldn't believe the Sorrel Drink was any cause for alarm, just like we didn't. We begged the officer to come inside and explain what happened, but all he did was tell our father, "Take it easy on them. They seem like good girls."

We darted inside and sprinted to our room like Usain Bolt. We locked the door and waited in fear all night. The officer's words must have had some effect - that or our dad could tell our fear was sufficient punishment - because we didn't see or hear from him until after school the next day.

He never did confront or discipline us. He might have known it was the Sorrel Drink after all.

On Valentine's Day, I received a note from a secret admirer. At the time, I had a huge crush on a boy named Jordan. I hoped it was from him, but it turned out Jordan had a girlfriend and no interest in me whatsoever. The Valentine was instead from my friend, Dave.

The note he wrote me was so sweet, I remember it to this day. He expressed his high school love for me in a way

I've never felt before or since, not even from my husband, especially my husband. But I was still bound by my father's law against boyfriends.

I was already helping my older sister hide her relationship. Leading a double life might have been in my blood, but it was too much for me to juggle.

I wasn't about to get the severe belt that was promised if my father found out. So, even though he'd pulled my attention away from Jordan with his sincere and beautiful words, I sadly checked the "no" box in answer to Dave's request to be my Forever Valentine.

CHAPTER 3

College

"Iron sharpens iron as one man sharpens another."

PROVERBS 27:17

High school went by in a flash, as things tend to do when you keep yourself busy. I had achieved everything I set out to accomplish in my school career.

The best part of the graduation ceremony was the looks on the bullies' faces as I was repeatedly called to the stage for awards and recognition. I beat them in academics, attendance, and conduct, and I would beat them in life. I proved to myself that God had my back when I trusted Him.

They say if you're the smartest person in the room, you should find a new room. They don't tell you how intimidating it is to enter the new room for the first time.

My first year at Seneca College was nerve-wracking. I was used to being seen as a sort of high-performance individual. Being surrounded by outgoing young adults whose grades were as good as mine made me feel inadequate and insecure.

One of the great mysteries of the universe is why I majored in marketing. My guidance counsellor and everyone else I knew suggested accounting because of my exceptional math skill, but there I was.

Of course, I was going to do it to the best of my ability. I stuck to my goals - hard work, no parties, and a part-time job to pay for school - for two years. And for two years, I was teased for studying alone in my room while everyone else went to parties.

In my second year, I started dating the most handsome man. He was a musician, so he'd usually be out late doing shows. I was so in love I wanted to spend every waking minute with him.

But then he started pressuring me to leave school. He said he wanted me to move in with him so we could one day start a family. I didn't know if he was joking or serious.

I told him I wasn't ready for that. How could I start a family and support children if I dropped out of college? And we were much too young anyway. I thought he'd understand because he cared about me. Instead, he started coming around less often.

I missed him, so I jumped on the subway to surprise him

at his mother's house. It went about as well as one would expect.

A couple on the train was putting on a pretty heavy public display of affection. Just as I thought *they should get a room*, they came up for air, and I saw that the man was my boyfriend.

It made sense, considering we were on the train to his mother's house. And that meant he was taking the girl home with him.

I turned away and moved to a spot on the train where he wouldn't see me. Instead of confronting him, I switched trains at the next stop and went home.

My roommate wasn't the nicest person in the world, so I didn't say anything when I got back. I just slid under my covers and cried my eyes out. He called me the next day, but I didn't answer. I never spoke to him again, and he probably still doesn't know why.

Soon after that, I met the man who would become my husband.

CHAPTER 4

Payroll

> *"May the God of hope fill you with all joy and peace in believing so that by the power of the Holy Spirit you may abound in hope."*
>
> ROMANS 15:13

After graduation, I got a public relations job and did some telemarketing. My job mostly involved feeble attempts to solicit donations from the elderly.

When my paycheques came in, they were always less than I expected based on my wage and hours worked. I didn't understand where my money was going. When I asked about it, I could never get a satisfactory answer.

My boss would dismiss my questions with vague answers about withholdings, taxes, and payments to this and that. I wanted an equation.

What *exactly* was happening to my money? I felt like I was being taken advantage of or ignored.

My career wasn't what I expected, and I had no passion for the work. I wasn't even interested enough to look for another job.

So immediately after getting my marketing degree, I started my education in payroll. If they weren't going to explain my paycheque, I'd figure it out myself.

Payroll immediately felt like a better fit for me. Maybe it was my proclivity for math or my determination to make sure I wasn't being taken for a ride with my pay. Either way, it felt like dropping a puzzle piece into its place.

I even studied HR up to the final exam. By then, I knew payroll was where my purpose and passion lived, so I forfeited the exam and missed my Chief Human Resources Leader designation.

While working on my payroll certifications at Seneca College, I worked for an international human resources software company.

It was an entry-level customer service position, but I was in the right field. My foot was in the door.

Then I found out I was pregnant.

Andre and I had been together for four years by now. He worked for a construction company making a decent wage.

He came to church with me now and then, and things

were moving in the right direction. We weren't married, but we knew we'd be together forever.

When I told him we were going to have a baby, he wasn't as excited as I had imagined.

I knew it would be a challenge, and I was scared too, but Andre almost seemed like he was upset with me. He told me, "We don't need kids yet. What are we going to do?"

I didn't get to experience a loving and supportive partner throughout my pregnancy.

No one rubbed my belly and smiled or mused with me about our child's great future. For the first time in my relationship, I felt very alone and neglected.

CHAPTER 5

Fired

> *"The Lord is a refuge for the oppressed, a stronghold in times of trouble."*
>
> PSALM 9:9-10

My father died in 2006 when I was five months pregnant. Andre was supportive, but now and then, I got the sense he was more worried about how this change would affect *his* life.

We moved to Ajax, a mid-sized town in the Greater Toronto Area. As soon as we were settled, I started looking for a new church. I tried many, but none felt quite right. Finally, a coworker invited me to join them at their church. I was in love less than ten minutes after the service started.

I was excited to hear the pastor preach. It felt so good to worship in the presence of God with people who truly loved Him as I did. I became a member and went back every Sunday.

Church was where I could enjoy myself the way many

people enjoy themselves at clubs or bars. I've been to a grand total of two nightclubs in my life. It was just never for me. Church is where I find the emotional relief and connection I need.

When Deondre was born, I reduced my school load from three weekly classes to one. It was slow-going, but I was still working at the same job, so we were okay.

I completed my Payroll Practitioner and Payroll Management Certification. I studied so much that by the time I finished school, I didn't just understand the ins and outs of my paycheque - I understood virtually every type of paycheque distribution process in Canada.

The best part was that it all felt right. I finally felt like I was moving in the right direction. I had taken a huge step toward my purpose - the path that God laid out for me and the reason he saved my life when I was so sick as a child.

I continued my education with advanced computer courses, seminars - basically any relevant knowledge I could get my hands on.

My employer took advantage of my growing expertise by moving me to different departments to teach the staff.

When a supervisor role became available, my Director

encouraged me to apply. My resume passed the initial screening, and I was called for an interview. However, when I got there, I was told there was a "conflict of interest," and I was fired.

With my shiny new certifications, I secured a higher-paying position as a senior payroll administrator. The drawback was that I had to commute three hours a day, and that took time and money I would have spent with Deondre and taking care of my household responsibilities.

I worked alongside a bitter secretary who went out of her way to make sure I understood she was my superior.

She would deliberately create hurdles in my work, like rushing non-urgent tasks in front of my deadlines. It wasn't long before I moved on to a similar position and started thinking about how nice it would be to do my job as a contractor instead of an employee.

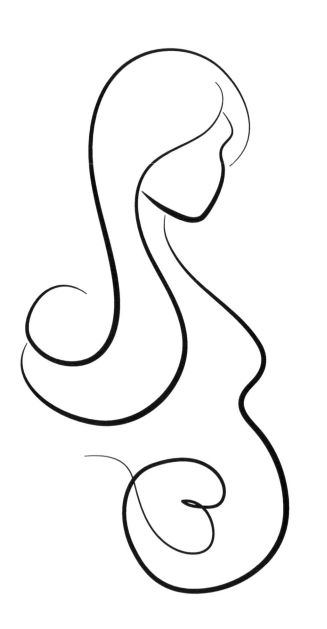

CHAPTER 6

Deondre

*"Children are a gift from the Lord;
they are a reward from him."*

PSALM 127:3

Deondre is an extraordinary child. He listens well and is dedicated to his studies. He maintained exemplary grades up until high school. Now that he's in French immersion, things are more challenging, but he still excels and impresses me daily.

He was christened in the Pentecostal church and would attend service with me on Sundays. This always annoyed Andre. In our early years, Andre would attend church with me now and then, but he didn't realize it would be so constant in my life.

Throughout my pregnancy, I felt that Andre was uninterested. However, when Deondre finally arrived, Andre was delighted at his freckles and toes and told his friends all about his beautiful baby boy.

He would take Deondre everywhere and spend much time at his mother's house. I felt like I didn't see much of Deondre when Andre was home from work.

It was nice to see Andre excited about his son, but things were difficult for me behind closed doors. He didn't spend much time bathing or feeding Deondre.

He didn't seem to worry about the domestic aspects of raising a child - or the domestic aspects of our lives in general - so it fell on me.

He would insist on dressing Deondre in flashy, expensive clothing so he could show him off. I preferred modest superstore clothes, but Andre would argue the point.

At home, they would play, and Andre would practice reading with him. I was grateful for that. Andre was hard on Deondre, rushing him through walking and potty training, then later in academics. It's difficult to say whether that stringency did him more harm than good.

Deondre was in daycare before he was six months old because I had to go back to work. He always cried when he had to leave Mommy.

He went through four childcare centers because of frequent accidents and refusal to eat. He only wanted Mommy's food.

And he would only come to me when he wanted

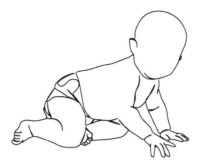

something because he knew Dad would be harsh.

Andre was the go-to guy at his construction job. He had to be gone a lot, or so he told me. He had a company car and would often leave before 6:00 A.M. and come home as late as 10:00 P.M.

When it was a special occasion, he'd tell me he'd be home at a specific time and show up hours later.

Because of my long commute, Deondre would be the first or second child at daycare - right when the doors opened - and he'd be one of the last to leave.

I'd pick him up, feed him, bathe him, put him to bed or to play, and be online for class in the evening.

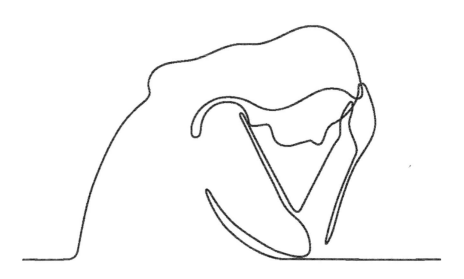

CHAPTER 7

Aneurysm

"And the prayer of faith shall save the sick, and the Lord shall raise him up; and if he has committed sins, they shall be forgiven him."

JAMES 5:16

One day in 2010, I woke up with a splitting headache. The pain was so intense I knew there must be something wrong. I went to the doctor.

After some tests and imaging, he diagnosed me with a "small, pouched aneurysm" in my brain. An aneurysm is a section of the arterial wall that has thinned and ballooned from the outward pressure.

Many of them rupture, causing potentially catastrophic bleeding. Almost half of those people die, and the rest often have neurological problems for the rest of their lives.

I was shocked and terrified. I could die or become disabled at any moment, and my odds of successful brain surgery weren't good enough.

At this point, I'd already seen some selfish and unpleasant behaviours from my boyfriend, but my life was at risk. I expected sympathy and support. Maybe some encouragement. Concern, at the very least.

When I told him, he didn't respond at all. He went about his day as if I'd just read him the weather report. I thought maybe he didn't understand what my diagnosis meant, but he didn't ask. He wasn't interested. He didn't ask if I was okay, if I needed him, or if I was scared. No, he flew his red flag high, and I ignored it.

Over the following weeks, I grew depressed. I cried night and day, fearing my life would be cut short any second. Deondre would become motherless because of some random roll of the medical malady dice. My bad luck.

I called Minister Small and asked him to pray with me. What he told me during that call has stayed with me. "You will live and not die. You will be there to raise your grandchildren."

His encouragement rekindled my fighting spirit. I stopped asking God why this was happening. I started trusting His plan.

CHAPTER 8

Family

"Anyone who does not provide for their relatives, and especially for their own household, has denied the faith and is worse than an unbeliever."

1 Timothy 5:8

That year, I made the worst mistake of my life. I had sponsored my mother and brothers' immigration to Canada because my mother was struggling financially, and she missed me and her grandson. The papers finally went through, and they came.

The mistake wasn't bringing them to Canada. The mistake was bringing them into our home. I loved having my family near me, but the dynamic between my family and my boyfriend was unsustainable.

Nevertheless, I couldn't afford an apartment, so they moved in, intending to find a place of their own.

My mom saw that Andre didn't cook, clean, or care for

Deondre much at home. She wouldn't say anything to him outright.

However, she would mumble or tell me in private that he treated me like a slave and neither did he show good behaviors of a good son-in-law. Despite her opinion, she never hesitated to help me.

My brothers were louder and generally more aggressive – toward each other and our mom.

When Andre told them to stop behaving that way, they would react with hostility toward him. They were hardheaded and wanted things to be their way.

My mom and brothers would talk to other people about how things were in our home, and word would get back to Andre.

He called them ungrateful and praised himself for everything he was doing for them. He twisted their words and used everything they said against them.

One day, my brother used Andre's shaver without asking his permission. In our culture, it's not a big deal.

Using something that belongs to someone else in your household, is accepted behaviour, but Andre was angry. I asked my brother to apologize and not do it again, but it seemed to me that Andre held a grudge.

He would hound them, watching how much they ate, how often they opened the refrigerator, who they spoke to on the phone, and what they talked about.

Then he would use that to berate me. I would respond by shutting down and going silent, but it was tearing me apart inside.

If my mom spoke to someone on the phone about something negative that happened back in her old neighbourhood, like crime or death, he would tell me that's where I come from. Those are my people, and that they are ungrateful. We're all the same. We talk the same. I'm just like them.

We became more determined to get them a place of their own. My mother-in-law had a friend with a vacant apartment, so we put them there.

I still heard the same criticisms and insults every day, but my family was happy, and there was less pressure.

My mom would come over sometimes to help me cook and clean. She made her opinion clear to me but got along with Andre fine. She was even friends with his mother for a time. That ended when his mother asked my mother, "Can you believe Garcia is spending all that money to have Deondre in soccer when I'm struggling to pay my rent? My son should be using that money to help me."

My late father's side of the family got along with Andre and tolerated his mother, but Andre's serious demeanour was off-putting to them. They couldn't tell whether he was joking or being rude when he interacted with them, but they'd get along for my sake most of the time.

CHAPTER 9

In-Laws

"Therefore shall a man leave his father and his mother, and shall cleave unto his wife: and they shall be one flesh."

GENESIS 2:24

My mother-in-law knew I didn't enjoy her company. My mother helped with the chores and made my life easier, whereas my mother-in-law would only insert herself and her opinion where they weren't welcome, but Andre would complain that my mother came over more than his.

We never went to my family events. There was always something going on with Andre's family. A birthday, a holiday, an announcement, a gift.

The straw that broke the camel's back was when Andre's brother and his girlfriend started bringing their niece over.

The pair of them liked to party, and they needed a

babysitter for their daughter, so they'd bring her to our house.

As the sole owner of the household duties, babysitting fell into my realm. Andre would even go with them sometimes and leave me with the girl.

They didn't pick her up on time, so we'd often have to take her home. They were just generally irresponsible, and I was tired of working as their hired help for free. It was an inconvenience to take an extra child everywhere I had to go, to cook for her, to do all the things her parents should have been doing.

When I finally told Andre I wouldn't be babysitting anymore; I was accused of not liking the little girl. I explained that whether I liked her was irrelevant.

What I didn't like was them taking advantage of me and taking me for granted. They were using me, and they didn't even like me!

They denied their entitled and audacious behaviour and continued to accuse me. I told Andre I didn't care what they thought. They were not to drop their child off with me again.

The story turned into "Garcia hates us," like a giant game of Telephone. My family kept to themselves while Andre's family gossiped, spied, pried, and plotted. It was enough to make anyone feel crazy.

His mom was one of those that clung to their sons, not allowing them to transition from son to husband. She refused to abdicate her role as the leading lady in his life. He encouraged her behaviour by inviting her into every discussion, argument, and plan.

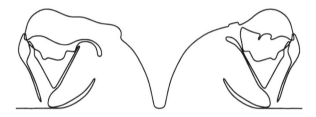

I became increasingly frustrated as she continued to insert herself into my parenting and relationship.

On one occasion, I put my foot down and said, "We're going on a family trip without your mother or your niece."

After that, my relationship with his mother turned sour. She would say negative things about me to the rest of her family, including my husband. She knew I didn't want her in my home, and she could see that Andre had to hide the things he gave to her and did for her.

Andre told me his mom loved me and feared me, but I never saw any indication of that. Her behaviour toward me never resembled anything like love from my perspective.

They became even more cold and bitter, and my

family developed the theory that they were jealous of my education. Also, the mother was jealous of the time I spent with her son.

CHAPTER 10

Baptism

"Repent and be baptized every one of you in the name of Jesus Christ for the forgiveness of your sins, and you will receive the gift of the Holy Spirit."

ACTS 2:38

When Deondre was five years old, we had a Swiss Chalet dinner together because I was more tired than usual. We were sitting on the couch watching his TV show when I started to feel ill. I went upstairs for a quick shower, hoping it would make me feel better, but I had severe vertigo. I washed quickly and returned downstairs to find my son right where I had left him.

I fell to the ground on my short walk back to the couch. I saw hell and screamed, "Lord, help me! My child needs me, and I need you!"

The next thing I knew, my house was host to paramedics and my neighbour, who was comforting my son.

I heard Deondre say, "Mom, don't die. The Swiss Chalet

food hurts you." I was grateful for his love and concern, but I knew it wasn't rotisserie chicken doing this to me.

I spent a few days in the hospital, listening to Andre explain how I was responsible for what happened to me. I should have eaten better and taken better care of myself.

I quietly asked God how I could eat healthily and adequately care for myself when all my time and energy belonged to my egotistical and unappreciative partner.

Things were getting steadily worse at home. I feared going out, spending money, or asking for things. Every day, I was blamed for something new.

I called my pastor and asked if I could be baptized. If there had ever been a time I needed strength from God, it was now.

After a short waiting period, I got the call that my baptism was approved. The weight seemed to fall immediately from my shoulders.

The next few days were the best I'd had in a long time. I felt protected. Invincible.

Pastor Brown started counselling me and teaching me about forgiveness. I listened intently to him and applied his lessons in different areas of my life, but the place I needed it most was the place I wasn't ready to share forgiveness just yet.

I say "share" because I learned that forgiveness isn't just something you give to another person; it's something you give yourself.

When you forgive, you drop the burden of hurt and anger. You let the problematic behaviour pass through you, see it objectively, and maybe you say a little prayer for the person who continues to sin against you.

But I wasn't there yet with my husband and his family. I was still hurt and angry, and it would be another ten years before I was ready to let that go and accept God's peace, love, and relief.

Over time, the sense of protection I got from my baptism faded. My partner grew increasingly controlling and dismissive. I asked God how He could allow a baptized follower to endure such trials. No answer. I asked so many questions, night after night, with no response.

I read the Bible, but it didn't orient me like it used to. I hardly understood what I was reading. I felt attacked and oppressed and far away from God. I knew without a doubt that I was the single most confused and lost person on the face of the Earth.

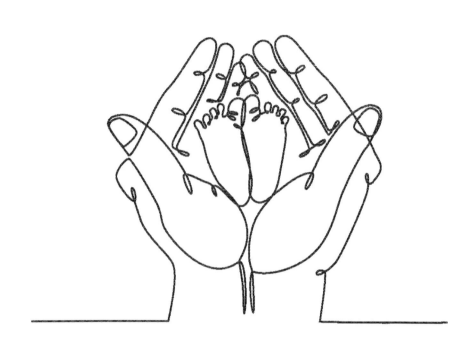

CHAPTER 11

Two

"We are hard-pressed on every side but not crushed, perplexed but not in despair, persecuted but not abandoned, struck down but not destroyed."

2 Corinthians 4:8-9

In 2012, I gave birth to my second son. We called him "the gifted child" because he was - and still is - a soccer prodigy.

Ceyon had his big brother Deondre to look up to, and he picked up on everything Deondre had learned over the years.

When Ceyon was two and a half, he was doing professional-level tricks with the soccer ball. Andre raved over Ceyon's skill and told everyone, "That's my boy! He's going to play soccer!"

Poor Deondre, who had been playing soccer and excelling academically for years, fell off Andre's radar.

I regret to admit I also let Deondre's soccer experience fall into neglect. But he was my scholar, and Ceyon was my athlete.

Ceyon started to play on junior league teams when he was four years old. Then he moved up to competitive league teams. Soon, he was playing on three competitive teams at once.

Today, at only ten years old, he plays for four teams and travels around Europe and North America for games and special training.

As much as he excelled in soccer, he rejected academics. He would say his homework was done when it wasn't and generally didn't care about his performance.

It seemed like Ceyon got away with things Deondre would never get away with. Andre would even allow Ceyon to talk back to him with no discipline.

We often argued about his favouritism, but he would just take offence and continue the same way.

When I wanted to take the boys to church, Andre was even more annoyed than before.

He would tell them church people were not good people and that I was wrong for forcing them to go.

He said I spent too much time in church. There were days he bullied me into staying home with him. On those

TWO

days, I'd refuse to speak to him.

I felt deliberately separated from my sanctuary just because he couldn't control me there. He wasn't able to represent himself as a benevolent caretaker.

Church had been a pillar of my existence longer than I'd ever known this man.

The more I appeased him, the more I lost myself, but I thought appeasing him was the only way to gain an ounce of peace. So, I bottled it up and prayed for change.

The in-laws started invading my house again because Andre didn't have time to visit his mom all the time now that he was chauffeuring for soccer practice and daycare.

By early 2013, I'd had enough. I gave Andre an ultimatum – he could live in this home with me, or he could live in this home with them.

If he didn't fix the situation, I'd leave and take the kids. He responded about how I expected him to.

So, I got a lawyer. We sold the house and split the profits, which gave me enough to buy a house of my own.

Andre would come by to pick up the kids. Nothing was changing. He was still lying and refusing to take responsibility for his behaviour. He still wasn't getting it. And I felt good here in my own space.

After about six months, he couldn't bear to be without his children anymore. He agreed to go to counselling and moved in with me in the home I bought for myself and my boys.

In one counselling session, I explained that we both work, but I'm the only one who regularly handles household responsibilities.

Andre told the counsellor, "Garcia doesn't have to work. She's just killing herself for no reason." For the millionth time, I explained that I didn't want to be a stay-at-home-mom, but Andre persisted.

The counsellor asked what he meant when he said I didn't have to work and said it would be chauvinistic if he indeed meant for me not to work at all if I wanted to.

We didn't make it to the separate individual counselling that was supposed to complement the couple's counselling.

TWO

Around this time, the in-laws started showing up at my house, always with an excuse about why they needed to be there.

Nothing had changed. We had the same fights we had in our previous home. The hostilities were just a little dampened but otherwise the same.

CHAPTER 12

Marriage

"Watch out for those who cause division or put obstacles in your way."

ROMANS 16:17

Andre and I were married when I was 34 years old. From the comfortable perspective I have now, I can see it was an obvious mistake to enter a marriage of an unequal yoke, but I wanted it for my children. Things were going well at the time.

He would show me off to everyone like he was proud. He would tell them about my education and brag that he had married the smartest woman. He told them I'd earn bundles of money and take care of him.

His family - like my family had seen years ago - became jealous of how he seemed to admire my prospects. They bad-mouthed me for "hating" them and treating them badly; for not liking Andre's niece or wanting his mom to practically live in my house.

I turned again toward God like David when Saul was after him. My health still waned. I got into accidents and fell ill frequently.

My support system had withered, and I spent most days crying and asking God for guidance.

My husband would harshly accuse me and blame me for anything and everything. It was my fault that Ceyon still sucked his thumb. It was my fault when my health was bad. When the kids were sick, that was my fault too.

I was the source of all his pain and stress, and yet, he was the one who followed me. Somewhere inside him, he knew I was the source of his security and comfort - not his pain and stress. I was just an easy target for his frustration.

His behaviour felt emotionally abusive to me, especially in front of our boys. It felt like he was trying to show them I was inferior.

It felt like he was showing them that women are inferior - and that the way he treated me was something to be admired and imitated.

I was disgusted, but I continued to be the obedient wife. That's what I knew to do. I did nothing to curb the behaviour or protect myself.

I just prayed and prayed often. I believed the hurtful things he'd tell me, and I blamed myself for things that weren't - that couldn't have been - my fault.

I thought this was a rough time that would pass. A storm. Someday, he was bound to realize it was better to honour and respect me as he promised in his vows.

I used to tell myself, "The stone the builder rejects all along becomes the cornerstone."

Eventually, it was too much. I needed help. I told Andre how stressed I was by his behaviour and his family's control over our relationship.

His response was to consult his mother and bring his family further into our marriage.

Nothing was going the way I'd imagined when I was younger. I blamed the devil for my struggles and cursed him to leave me alone.

In those days, I reminded myself of Job. Job was a wealthy property owner with four children and loved God. God even praised his virtue in front of the devil. So the devil tested him.

When his children and livestock were dead, his wealth and property gone, and he was dying covered in painful skin lesions, Job questioned God.

He thought God was punishing him, and he wanted to

know how anyone could please Him without the capacity to understand His ways. However, this was not the end of Job's story. Job, after everything he had endured, remained faithful to God.

In the end, Job praised God even without His favour and protection, so God restored Job's health and wealth and blessed him with even more property and more children.

Job showed us that suffering doesn't mean God is punishing us. Suffering can mean He's allowing the devil to give us an opportunity to rise.

I struggled ceaselessly with my in-laws, living in a constant state of unease and discomfort. They'd smile to my face and then say the worst things about me to my husband and amongst themselves.

He would tell me it was all in my mind or I shouldn't worry about what everyone said, even though it was him - my partner - joining in the conversation. They would even feign friendship with me just to pry into my marriage.

Their attacks were often so bad I was tempted to physically hurt them when things got heated.

When I was angry, I wanted to tear them apart, and I knew I could. I imagined the satisfaction of giving them what I believed they deserved.

I even considered running away from the situation to stop myself from doing something I'd regret.

But instead, I kept my peace and kept my mouth shut. I blamed the world, the devil, and my husband, but I was the one allowing the treatment to continue.

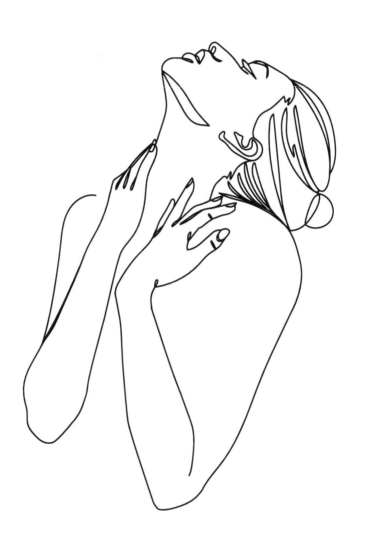

CHAPTER 13

Health

"Is there no balm in Gilead?"

JEREMIAH 8:22

There hadn't been any change in my health in five years, even though I'd been attended by a neurologist and an endocrinologist the whole time. Throughout those years, I never stopped praying. I called upon the Blood of Christ and engaged in daily devotionals. I often fell to my knees, crying out to God.

At a routine MRI, a triage nurse carelessly asked me, "Oh, you're here for the follow-up about the cancer?" My mouth fell open, and I stared at her. Did she think I was someone else or was I about to be told I had cancer on top of an aneurysm? While I waited for the doctor, I desperately wondered what would happen to my children if I died. I prayed silently, "Father God, you are the most high God."

The doctor was young and uninterested in my consultation. Surely he was in a hurry to get through a

long list of patients crammed into a tight schedule that day. I told God this was not the place for me and that I would live and not die. The doctor reviewed my images and told me everything looked good. He said I could follow up in a few years. He spent less than five minutes with me and changed my life forever.

My pastor worshipped with me over the phone after my consultation. A few days later, I received a call from the neurologist. He confirmed that there was no longer an aneurysm. Just a small, shrinking bump.

Looking back, it's clear that I was being tested. My children were often sick throughout my illness, and there were constant battles with my husband. It was a turbulent and strenuous time. I thanked God and promised Him that I would keep fighting.

CHAPTER 14

Business

"Wealth gained hastily will dwindle, but whoever gathers little by little will increase it."

PROVERBS 14:23

With all my renewed energy, I decided to start a payroll business. It was an idea I'd tossed around since 2011 with minimal progress. I registered my business as a sole proprietorship, bought a domain, and created a logo. My logo was cheap - very "homemade" looking - and it told the world I wasn't serious or professional. But there was no money for design or advertising.

In 2018, my husband expressed interest in starting a cabinet design and manufacturing business. We devised a plan to put my business aside and get his up and running. When we had more money for marketing and such, we'd turn our attention back to my business.

On top of my household duties, I worked constantly to support us while he built his company, established a reputation, and grew a customer base.

We never turned our attention back to my company. He was satisfied to work his job, not help at home, and not help me with my business, even while I handled his HR, accounting, and payroll in addition to my full-time job and domestic duties.

He wouldn't even give me an opinion on the work I was doing on my own. I asked him what he thought of my website, which I had professionally designed, and he didn't respond. He would give it a quick glance and nothing more. He would say he supported me, but beyond his words, there was nothing.

He brushed off all of my attempts to get myself going, so I would handle everything on my own all day long, and at the end of the day, I would settle in to work on my business. My husband would ask, "Aren't you coming to bed?" as if he hadn't even heard me tell him what I was doing.

I found myself pouring out to God. I pleaded with Him to steer me in the right direction. I knew I had what it took to be successful. I devoted myself to payroll education to ensure I was the best. I knew every detail like the back of my hand. I developed a network of effective HR professionals to give my clients everything they needed. It was my turn.

In 2019, armed with nothing but a small credit card, I reached out to a marketing agency. I almost fell out of my

 seat when they told me the price, but I gave them the green light. I didn't have the money, but I had the faith. I signed the contract and exhausted my credit to pay the bill.

While the marketing team worked, I started the compliance process and reached out to many different banks. Some of them were lovely and simply couldn't provide the service I needed. Others gave me the impression I would have been accepted if I were a man. They asked questions like, "Don't you have kids," or, "Doesn't your husband work?"

One service provider told me, "Unless you're making millions, we can't offer you our services." Others told me they couldn't work with a business that had "payroll" in the company name. They said I was a huge risk to them. When I asked where my competitors started before they made millions, they brushed me off.

I was forced to find different avenues to conduct my business with dignity. The misogyny just made me more determined. They were the same as the bullies in high school and my husband at home. They underestimated me. I knew the most effective way to reject their behaviour was to be successful despite it.

With a new logo and some expertly targeted advertising

in place, I was in business. A slow trickle of clients was coming in, and I grew confident enough to pitch to my family. I received a government grant and used it to hire my first staff member, who was followed by more hires in different departments as we expanded.

CHAPTER 15

Twins

"When you pass through the waters, I will be with you; and through the rivers they shall not overwhelm you; when you walk through the fire you shall not be burned, and the flame shall not consume you."

Isaiah 43:2

In the midst of all that buckling down and building my business, I got news that spurred me to get serious and make my dream work sooner rather than later.

We went on a family vacation to Jamaica – just the four of us. Getting ready for the beach, I realized my bathing suit barely fit me. No big deal. I hadn't worn it in a while.

I sat around feeling nauseous and bloated while Andre played with Ceyon. Deondre mostly stayed with me. When we left the beach to get dinner, I didn't want to eat a thing. Everything I looked at put me off my appetite.

When I finally ate something just to calm my stomach, I threw it up minutes later.

Even with all these signs, I was floored when the doctor back home told me my urinalysis was positive for human chorionic gonadotropin (hCG) - the pregnancy hormone.

The urine test was confirmed by a blood test and later an ultrasound, but the ultrasound revealed two other things: I was carrying twins, and one of them was dead.

We scheduled a follow-up ultrasound two weeks later to ensure things were progressing as they should. When a twin dies, it isn't like when a single fetus dies. They don't usually have to be evacuated. The body - and the other twin - will reabsorb the tissues and use that energy to grow stronger.

I went home and told my husband. Andre's reaction was much like his reaction to anything else that was important to me.

I had another ultrasound done in two weeks but had to wait two more weeks to get the report. When I went to the clinic to get it, the doctor said, "I'm so sorry, Garcia. I misread the first ultrasound. Your babies are both healthy. You're going to have twins!"

For a second time, I was dumbstruck. I remember sitting in the car, trying to remember how to turn it on.

I cried all the way home - for joy, fear, and shock. When I told Andre, he said, "Are you sure that's what the doctor said? What are we going to do? Now we have to get a bus."

TWINS

In front of other people, he sounded excited and proud that he was such a man he could make twins. At home, there was no change. Business as usual.

I started prenatal care and prayed for girls. I would talk to God about how different life would be with girls. I dreamed about going shopping together and doing girl things.

I became hopeful and excited, but my five-month ultrasound revealed two boys.

I left Dr. Ma's office slightly disappointed. I even got a 3D ultrasound to confirm, but there were definitely no girls in there.

My husband and older boys were disappointed too. They had hoped for one boy and one girl. After the surprise wore off, we all agreed what mattered was that we were having two healthy babies.

When the twins came, I took maternity leave. With the extra time at home, I could be more productive with all the prep work for my company.

I put my fear aside and started telling people about it. I told the church, called my family and friends, and put display ads on buses and other things.

Andre would see my ads and get upset that I hadn't told him about this and that, but I'd play it off and keep grinding.

I didn't sleep when the twins slept. I worked. Deondre would help me watch them while he did his homework. Both boys adjusted and bonded quickly with the twins.

Deondre was 13, and Ceyon was 7, so they were able to help out with some things, especially when COVID came.

In 2020, my workload exploded exponentially. Remote learning for the boys on top of two new babies, working my regular job from home, and building a business in my "spare" time. I never got a break.

This was a time of complete devotion and sacrifice. It was difficult, and it was painful at times, but I knew I was flying full speed in the right direction.

I'd wake up at 5:00 A.M. to get lunch and snacks ready.

Then I'd get the twins ready for the drive to the older boy's schools.

When we got back from dropping them off, I'd work and take care of the twins. I worked right up until it was time to pick the boys up from school.

They finished at different times, so by the time I got back from picking them up, it was time to make dinner. Then we'd have just enough time to eat before soccer practice.

On the weekends, I'd take the boys to soccer games, handle the household chores, shop for groceries, do the laundry, prepare the meals, and go to church.

When I couldn't fit everything in, Andre would take one of the boys to soccer, or we'd ask another soccer parent to help. Most days, I felt like the worst mom because all I did was work.

I didn't have time to give my kids my full attention. This was a week after my cesarean delivery.

Andre told me he was working because there were many issues with projects, but when he came home, he would spend most of his time on the phone.

He claimed to be checking emails or something work-related.

He would see me bustling around and say, "Look at my robot wife. You should sit down."

I would answer, "If I sit down, what are the kids going to eat for dinner?" He'd look exasperated and say, "Okay, Garcia," but instead of getting up and offering to help with something, he'd just leave me to my chores.

I started bringing my mom over on the weekends to help cook and clean while I worked. Everything was teetering on the edge of overwhelm.

Every night, when the children went to sleep, I'd rush to my computer. I'd ask God why I was living like a single parent.

I'd pray for strength and focus, and I'd pour myself into my work with all the determination I could muster.

Everything I did was deadline-driven. Even when I was able to carve out a minute to spend with my children, I couldn't be fully relaxed and engaged.

I found myself yelling at them too often because I felt like I was doing everything alone. I was, in fact, doing everything myself, but my frustration was aimed in the wrong direction.

I felt like we were Andre's possessions, something tucked away and ignored, like an old picture on the wall.

He didn't feel the need to be consistently emotionally invested in our lives. His job was done. He married the woman and made the babies. His name would go on.

The positive side of COVID was that I grew further in my walk with God. My faith blossomed.

I talked to Him constantly, asking for protection and guidance and thanking him for our many blessings.

I began to think of Him as my business partner, an essential part of my professional - and personal - success.

My commitment to Him grew stronger every day, and I read the Bible with renewed vigour.

If I didn't understand a passage, I Googled an explanation. Reading His Word every day taught me - and continues to teach me - how to interact with people around me, including my children.

One day, I watched the kids play, thinking about how I'd do anything for them. I wondered how many other mothers were going through a similar situation.

There was no way I was the only one. They needed help just like I did, and I could help them.

Relief and contentment washed over me. I realized God knew exactly what he was doing when he sent the twins and made everything just a little bit harder. I'd be fulfilled if I could help just one mother break free from oppression. I knew my purpose. I prayed for the ability to make a difference with my work. I asked God to make me a vessel of hope through which His Word would spread.

Mothers out there were looking for independence through entrepreneurialism, but they needed support, and I was going to be there.

CHAPTER 16

Secrets

"Blessed is the one who perseveres under trial because, having stood the test, that person will receive the crown of life that the Lord has promised to those who love Him."

JAMES 1:12

Back in 2012, the year Ceyon was born, Pastor Brown taught me lessons about forgiveness and how it can heal and empower you. At the time, I wasn't ready to apply that lesson where it was most needed in my life.

But as we entered 2021, I started seeing more and more that the power my husband and my in-laws had over my anxiety and happiness was completely and irrevocably my decision.

The feeling that Andre was going to deliberately sabotage my business plans was growing stronger. I questioned my sanity and asked myself if I was being paranoid.

However, the way he dismissed me when I tried to show him things and then slithered around on his own to try to figure out what I was doing made me wary.

I started working in secrecy. I hid everything from my husband and his family. They would try to look over my shoulder and then have hushed conversations about my activities.

But I was finished giving my life to them. God had been pulling me in this direction all my life, and I was finally giving my life to Him.

When the kids began hybrid learning (part-time in the classroom), I started studying more.

If I wasn't reading the Bible, I reviewed payroll changes and other ideas in the virtual space. Learning and gaining expertise in my field made me excited for the future.

I was still doing my husband's HR, accounting, and payroll, but I eased the burden on myself by hiring someone to handle the receipting and such.

Andre told me I didn't need anyone for that, but he didn't see me. He didn't know - and he had no interest in knowing - how hard I worked to keep him and the kids comfortable while following my calling. So I hired them anyway.

One night, after a particularly bad fight with him, I drove off with tears in my eyes. All the resolve in the world couldn't stem the pain that comes with having a partner who doesn't truly love you.

I stopped in a shady neighbourhood, but I didn't care. I sobbed and asked God for a sign that He loved me. Anything at all. If God loved me, one human man wouldn't matter much.

A bright light shone in my rearview mirror. It was coming closer. It looked like a car trying to pass, so I just waited. They were approaching slowly, too slowly. I thought it was time to go, so I started my car. The light got close and stopped. It was so bright; I couldn't see the car or anything else around it. Just one solid mass of light stood behind my car.

I thought perhaps they noticed I had turned on my car, and they were politely letting me pull out in front of them. I looked away from the light to put my car in gear, and when I looked up, it was gone. No car, no one standing there with a flashlight or a phone. Nothing. Chills ran through my body, and I knew what I had seen.

I thanked God for the sign. When I got home, I dove back into my Bible. I was relieved and excited. I understood I had the power to renew my faith and make it larger than life - make it a formidable force of protection around me. God was here with me, and no one could knock me down.

CHAPTER 17

Melane

"Listen to advice and accept discipline, and at the end you will be counted among the wise."

PROVERBS 19:20

I took a turn when I met Melane. I was searching online for resources that might help me learn to run my business more effectively, and I came across an ad about women's confidence in business. I think the ad was about Melane's book, *Lemonade*.

I shared her Instagram post ad and reached out to her immediately. She got back to me and shared her pricing.

Once again, it was too expensive, but I couldn't afford *not* to do it. After one short conversation with her, I took the chance, and it paid off.

Melane took me from a scrambling mother to a strategized and organized business owner - and mother.

She gave me the confidence to stop giving everyone a discount just because they were pleasant or because I knew them. I became more comfortable speaking about my business and pitching it to other business owners.

She shared resources, literature, encouragement, information, and business savvy. I was networking more and praying when things got hard - but things were getting hard less often.

She taught me to block out negativity around me and not give it space. We reviewed my daily processes and made them more efficient, so I could get more done.

The program consisted of weekly coaching and continuing education three times per week. I was taking my boys with me to church and to program events.

Bringing them into my happiness and spending more time with them brightened my spirit.

Some of the literature Melane shared with me was about emotional intelligence.

It's interesting how much a person can be ignorant of without knowing it. What they say is not true.

Ignorance is not bliss. Developing my emotional intelligence was an eye-opener. I could see myself more clearly and understand my thought processes. That clarity gave me the tools to better manage myself and my reactions.

I could also see and understand the emotional processes that were happening in other people. I realized that how people express their emotions isn't always indicative of their feelings.

This new knowledge made my positive relationships stronger, more comfortable, and more meaningful.

In my less-than-great relationships, I could look at situations and behaviours objectively and be content with controlling what I could control.

Another book Melane shared with me taught me to visualize my success.

I learned to offboard the people who would only doubt me or stand in my way and onboard people who would actively, honestly support me.

I found that there were far too many people who were smiling to my face but secretly against my success.

For as long as I live, I will never forget Melane and what

she did for me. Being confident in my skills in front of prospects and asking for what I'm worth has changed my professional life for good.

The ability to observe a negative - even hateful - behaviour and not be emotionally devastated, to only feel pity for the actor, and to continue doing what's good for my children and me ... that's invaluable.

CHAPTER 18

Forgiveness

"For if you forgive other people when they sin against you, your heavenly Father will also forgive you."

Matthew 6:14

One day, my husband's mother and sister went off on me. They were being aggressive and hateful. I wanted to knock them both on their tails or, at the very least, verbally defend myself, but I didn't. I waited. When my spouse told me they were right - that I deserved the verbal assault - I finally got the message loud and clear.

Their opinion wasn't going to be the highest priority anymore - not for me. If he wanted to make his entire life about their preferences and whims, he was free to do so.

The lessons from Melane and Pastor Brown came together at the perfect time, undoubtedly according to God's design. I was ready and had the emotional and professional tools I needed.

It was the hardest thing I've ever done, and it took more than a decade, but I forgave my husband for how he treated me.

I took Pastor Brown's words to heart and decided to give Andre and his family only kindness. What they said or did didn't matter anymore. It didn't  matter if they chose to be angry or resentful or say bad things about me.

This is my home, and their behaviour doesn't change that. Just as my pastor tried to tell me ten years prior, that release - that forgiveness - has set me free. I would no longer be afraid or have anxiety and panic attacks over their abuse. They weren't going to stop me from reaching my goals. I deleted their contact information from my phone and leaned into my company without a single backward glance.

Over the following months, I saw a calmer and happier version of myself emerge. I was seeing life differently. My inspiration to help other people filled me with energy.

I could see now that forgiveness was a gift to myself, and I had more patience for those who lacked understanding.

I forgave my husband. He was going to be the husband and father he was, and nothing I did would change that.

So, I let go of my pain and anger and regret. I would keep my vows because that's who I am before God, and what my husband did with his vows was his business.

CHAPTER 19

Future

"And we know that for those who love God all things work together for good, for those who are called according to his purpose."

Romans 8: 28

In September 2022, I discovered my mother has amyotrophic lateral sclerosis, also known as ALS or Lou Gehrig's Disease.

ALS is a degenerative nerve disease that affects the brain and spinal cord, causing progressive loss of motor function and paralysis until the person can no longer breathe on their own.

Then, they're either put on a ventilator or allowed to die. On a ventilator, they may live an extra five years. In all cases, the brain's ability to control voluntary movement is eventually completely inhibited. Her disease has progressed to the "moderate" stage. She's been sick for over three years now. It's hard to understand her speech sometimes.

A few fingers, on one hand, don't work as they should, but she can still use the hand. She can walk but has difficulty picking up one leg to get into a car, so she has to lift it with her hands.

They put her on some medications to slow it down and advised us of the importance of massage and exercise. I take her to massage and other appointments on my lunch break while the kids are at school.

She's much happier than she would be if she were just sitting around wasting away. I'm grateful for that. Sometimes she tells me, "I don't have this disease. I'm going to get better. I'm going to heal." I do my best to only be positive for her.

When I told Andre, he surprised me with some compassion. I was crying, and he said, "I'm so sorry. Why did this have to happen to *her*?" Then he forgot about it and never offered to help me get her to her many appointments or followed up about her health.

I pray for him. My brothers reacted much the same.

I'm going to push through. I'll take care of my mother and husband and children. I'll call my family for help when I need it and lean on God. I know God will help me manage and have everything I need because I always have.

You might be asking, "Why don't you just leave?" I don't

believe in divorce, but it goes beyond that. My parents were never married, so it's not like the idea of children outside of marriage appalls me. But I have several reasons to stay, and these reasons matter immensely to me. I took vows. I made promises before God and the church. Even if my husband fails to uphold his vows, I still have to uphold mine.

God gave me love and the ability to forgive. I must share that love and forgiveness with those who need it most.

Andre has a problem with himself. I fear he can't love the kids and me the way he should.

As I studied emotional intelligence, I started to see indications of a psychological need to make himself seem important the same way his mother does. That compulsion probably goes back generations.

God might change him, and He might not, but that's not for me to worry about. Our children will suffer if we divorce. When we used to fight, Deondre would cry, and Ceyon wouldn't eat. They suffered the most out of any of us. But we don't fight anymore.

To anyone asking, "Why do you stay in a marriage that makes you unhappy?" I'm not unhappy anymore. I'm not hurting. I don't fight with him, even when he tries. He and his family have no power over me anymore, and they never will again.

My business is thriving, my children are healthy, and when Andre does something that used to hurt me, I take the opportunity to "forgive and let live" and let my blessings flow.

You're going to go through things that hurt. That's the reality. You're going to be bruised and battered. You're going to feel loss and betrayal. If you're climbing toward success, it will not come easy.

But the answer is never to run away. *Faith is the substance of things hoped for, the evidence of things not seen.* Cling to God and push through.

As for me, I'm in the garden, and it's my turn to reap.

Garcia Hanson-Francis

Garcia Hanson-Francis is a resilient woman who made a decision to fight for her passion. She graduated with a diploma in Marketing and several certifications in Payroll Management, Bookkeeping, and related specialties. She also studied right up to the exam for HR designation but walked away to focus on payroll.

Garcia also has a passion for helping her community, particularly women who are fighting for success just like she did. In 2019, she launched a Virtual Tax Clinic that files tax returns for underprivileged community members. The clinic is one of her most cherished professional activities and accomplishments to date.

Garcia Hanson-Francis, CPM, is the CEO of CADJPro Payroll Solutions Inc., which she founded in 2020.

Outside of the professional world, Garcia loves to cook, and she's good at it! She's passionate about learning the Word of God every single day. After battling illness and circumstance throughout her life, Garcia realized her loyalties had been misplaced. Through prayer and fasting, she was able to put herself back together and make herself available for the blessings God had in store for her.

AWARDS

- Top 20 Outstanding Women CEOs of 2022 by Women Leaders Magazine
- The Most Admired Women Leaders in Business 2022, Inc. Magazine
- Founding Member of Immigrant Women in Business
- RBC Women of Influence Nominee
- Most Iconic Women Leaders, Excelligent Magazine
- ByBlacks Peoples Choice Award Winner, in 2020 and 2021 (Accounting Category)

TO CONTACT GARCIA:
(647) 762-2235
E: info@cadjpro.com
www.cadjpro.com

Testimonials

JACKIE WILLIAMSON, RN, BScN, MED, PH.D.
PROFESSOR, PRACTICAL NURSING PROGRAM

My relationship with Garcia carries different roles - mother, sister, best friend, confidant, mentor, and advisor. We switch between these roles and provide support for each other depending on what we are going through.

Her motivation to be the best at her career while also being the best wife and mother is a position that black women are historically expected to cope with regardless of their physical or mental health.

Garcia has consistently demonstrated high ethical mannerisms, personally and professionally. Sharing her story to help another person, especially another woman of colour, is necessary and important today.

VYNIQUE CHARLTON, COLLEGE FRIEND

Garcia has often said she's a boring person. That is far from the truth. She was never one to go clubbing or drinking. She was the one who enjoyed a good sports game and exploring Toronto with me. She even accompanied me on my first subway ride. I will always cherish the memory of our college days.

I remember Garcia always made sure I wasn't spending the holidays alone. She knew I was an international student. When I wasn't travelling home for the holidays, I was invited to dinner with her and her family.

Over the years, I nicknamed her 'Lady G' because she is so poised. She called me 'Baby Girl' because she was - and still is - a big sister to me. She taught me to love myself. She taught me to constantly work on improving myself in the service of God and those we cross in life.

Garcia is my friend, a friend whose virtues of grace, humility, wisdom, and kindness continue to flow with abundance to everyone she meets. She's a woman who has shown up for her family unwaveringly. She loves God, and she leads by example.

"Stay blessed, Lady G."

Pastor Lance Brown

I am Pastor Lansfield Brown, Pastor of the Refuge City Pentecostal Church located in Ajax Ontario. I have had the privilege and the pleasure of knowing Garcia for the past 12 years. I came to know her when she made a commitment to follow the Lord Jesus Christ in one of our worship services. She continues to keep that vow to the Lord in spite of life's challenges. She is acquainted with the Word of God and knows how to apply it in her daily life.

Garcia is a dedicated wife and mother of four lovely children; she makes it her point of duty to invest quality time in the lives of all her children. She is what you call a "soccer mom." She believes in her children's ability and takes the time to nurture it. She also knows the importance of *"Training up a child in the way he should go: and when he is old, he will not depart from it"* (Proverbs 22:6). She demonstrates this by being proactive in their education, temporal and spiritual.

At a personal level, Garcia is an industrious, disciplined person with a pleasant personality. She is not afraid of challenging work, and as an entrepreneur, business-minded person who is motivated to learn new material, and to offer her service to her community. This is a great quality of Garcia's.

It is my prayer that she continue to commit her ways to the Lord so that He will continue to direct her path.

Sonny Sidhu, HR Manager

I met Garcia in early March 2019, when I was recruiting for a Senior HR Generalist for CST Consultants Inc. From the moment I met Garcia and began to interview her for the role, I instantly knew that she would be the one that I would be hiring. Garcia spoke from her heart, and I could tell that she was confident in her abilities. After hiring Garcia, I resigned and only had the opportunity to work with her for a short while.

During this time, I realized that I had made the correct decision and that Garcia would be the right person for the business. She excelled immediately and began to learn a very complicated process quickly. As I moved on, I stayed in touch with Garcia, and we'd discuss matters ranging from her family to work.

Garcia always came across to me as a family-first individual who is committed to ensuring that her family is supported and that their needs are put first. At the same time, she takes great pride in what she does professionally, and she does it well!

I have been fortunate to know her these past three years and hope that we can continue our relationship.

Devon Goulbourne, Assistant Pastor, R.C.P.C

I have known this young lady, for the past 18 years. During this time, she has proven herself to be a very loyal and trustworthy friend. Garcia is one of the kindest and most compassionate people you will ever meet.

She is a young woman of high character and integrity who loves the Lord Jesus Christ, her family, and her friends. She is a very hard worker with a tremendous work ethic, as evidenced by the fact that she not only runs a business but helps her husband run his business, along with being a full-time mom to four young children. She is highly intelligent, resourceful, and ambitious, and she knows what she wants, and nothing will stand in the way of achieving her goals.

Garcia has touched so many lives, and I can proudly say I am one of them. My life has been enriched since I met my dear friend Garcia and I know that this friendship will continue for many years to come just because of the genuine individual she is. I have the utmost love, respect and admiration for Garcia, and I cherish our friendship beyond measure.

Andrea Watson, Friend from school days

I've known Garcia for many years. How did we meet? Well, I met Garcia at a Customer Care call centre, in downtown Toronto, about 20 years ago. We were full-time students working in a full/part-time customer service sales position. Our shifts were long, but we were determined to meet our targets each day. I was immediately drawn to Garcia's bubbly personality. She is a down to earth, God fearing, beautiful, strong, smart, educated, competitive, fashionista and sweet as pie.

A couple of years later into our friendship, Garcia confided in me that she and Andre were pregnant and ready to build a future together.

She was established in her career and ready for what God had in store. What was pretty awesome after finding out that she was going to be a mother was that day she gave birth. Her first child and I share the same birthdate! I was so thrilled and excited about her family expansion. Now there are four loves, truly a blessing.

We have the same passion for personal growth and development. I admire her striving for excellence. Garcia has built a career in Payroll, designated Payroll Manager, and owns and runs a successful business that helps many business owners. I am so proud of her and wouldn't expect anything less.

Our working relationship turned into a great friendship. We often talked about our walk with Christ, challenges, goals, and aspirations. We approach various subjects on a personal level regarding marriage, family, and business. Garcia has never been afraid to tell the truth, and give her thoughts and opinions.

Anyone would respect her authenticity. It's hard to stand in your truth when you're being pressured by family, friends, or colleagues.

This is something so many people struggle for years to

learn. Everyone's journey in life is different, and that's okay. She knows herself and the choices she is comfortable making and the level of commitment to each deeply personal decision.

In some of our saddest moments in her life, some of the happiest times were when she was focused on her personal relationship with Christ and her family. It all comes from within. She has always approached the situation that we have no reason to feel like we are lacking, just because it didn't go the way we wanted it to. God is our provider and sustainer. All things are done through Christ, not in our own strength. If she had caved to every whim or pressure trying to discourage her or make her feel bad, she would be lost. When you're confident in your life path, it brings purpose and wholeness. Our friendship was just the same and stood the test of time.

We've been miles apart for over 10 years. I moved to the USA, but time nor distance could not separate our friendship.

Reconnected, we are still committed to God, helpings others, family, love, joy and peace, and life-time achievements (this is one of them). Congrats on the book.

Minister Sean Small, VOK Ministries

Garcia is a family person; she goes above and beyond to make sure her family is okay. She's one of the strongest people I know. To watch her deal with her family in the midst of dealing with pain, trauma and difficulties, is absolutely beautiful to look at. She's also a kind person. I can remember during times of difficulties in my life, she was there to help. Just thinking about it now, makes one want to emulate those qualities.

She loves God, juggling family, hard times and dealing with pure pressure is not easy; but I watch her face, and she still keeps the faith. I'm delighted to be a friend and as she would oftentimes say, a big brother. She's truly someone to look up to. Her outlook on life is amazing.

She works hard, I mean extremely hard! She's always looking for ways to make her and her family's life bigger and better, a thinker and worker indeed. She just lights up any room she enters. She makes a huge impact on lives, more than she even realizes. She is always so helpful (smh), I mean very helpful. I will always appreciate our friendship. She is as beautiful on the inside as on the outside. I will always love and appreciate my little sister, Garcia.

Melane Mullings
Award-winning, #1 bestselling author, business management consultant, and founder of Aere Management Consulting

Garcia's testimony of resilience through her 'life lemon' experiences is inspirational! The purpose God has blessed her with has empowered her to share the lemonade of her success with many. A transformational read that will leave you encouraged, inspired, and blessed.

Garcia's amazing determination and dedication to learn and apply the concepts shared during our business consulting sessions together is impressive and rare. Watching her journey has richly blessed me, and I wish her all the best personally and professionally as she continues to grow, and create exponential impact in the world for God's glory!

Conclusion

When you open a soda can and take a drink, you don't wonder what's inside. You just know, and there's no doubt. That's what faith feels like to me. Instead of questioning the Lord, I trust what He's ordained for me, and I allow Him to make the decisions in my life.

> *"Complete the past to embrace the future."*
> –Jack Canfield

I've used Jack Canfield's methods to express my anger, hurt, and fear and move toward understanding, forgiveness, and love. I had to let go of the animosity and pain to allow God's blessings into my life. It wasn't doing me any good to hold on to the pain and resentment. It drained the energy I should have been applying to my professional and personal success.

The next big thing takes time. It requires a process. But the blessings are in our hands, and there's nothing the enemy can do to steal them away.

Choose to accept better and don't allow unnecessary negativity to become familiar in your life.

Maybe your pain is still fresh. Maybe forgiving them right now feels like letting them off the hook for all the awful things they've done to you. Maybe you don't know what a relief it will be when you decide to let it go.

When you forgive, you're putting yourself back in the present, where good things can happen to you. Jack Canfield wrote that holding onto the past will *"rob you of the power you need to forge ahead in creation of what you want."*

Another quote that keeps me facing forward is from Nelson Mandela. He said, *"Resentment is like drinking poison and hoping it will kill your enemies."*

It's uncomfortable to face the things that aren't working, to look at them head-on with objective, analytical eyes. It starts with telling yourself the truth. Be honest and watch how things start to improve. Fight the fear and anxiety that has you trapped.

Not everyone in your life is put there to make things pleasant or easy, and not everyone is meant to stay forever. Some people are meant to be with you for only a season, and some will teach you difficult lessons before they go.

As you rise, some won't be able to stomach your altitude. Accept the steep climb God set before you, and allow those others to fall away.

Not every relationship is going to have a happy ending. When you're in an unhappy marriage, it's impossible to know for sure whether divorce will make you happier. What good is it if you're still miserable? Keep God in your midst, and you'll know whether to stay or leave.

Your purpose is bigger than your fear. Acknowledge and celebrate it. You are worth it. Brian Tracy said,

"Life is like a combination lock. Your job is to find the right numbers in the right order so you can have anything you want."

Decide what you want your future to look like. Believe it will happen, and take action. Your success is in your hands.

Tell yourself right now you will not allow your past, your resentment, or your mistakes to break you. Embrace your blessings.

Isaiah 41:13

For I the Lord thy God will hold thy right hand, saying unto thee, 'Fear not. I will help thee.'

Favourite Quotes from Martin Luther King:

"Don't allow anyone to pull you so low as to make you hate them." Don't allow even those that are close to you to make you feel like you are nobody. You should always feel like you count, always feel that you have significance, and always feel that your life has ultimate worth.

"You must have determination to achieve excellence in your various fields of endeavour." When you figure out what you're going to be in life, set out to do it as if the Lord called you at this particular moment in history to do it.

If you were called to scrub toilets or sweep floors, that's okay, do it like Michael Angelo painted pictures, do it like Shakespeare wrote poetry and do it like Beyonce, who sings her heart out.

Favorite Quotes from Jamie Kern Lima:

"Believe in the power of your microphone." You decide who you want to turn up or turn down the volume on. You may have a friend or partner that you absolutely love, but as soon as you share your dreams with them, they turn negative and that sucks your energy.

Don't be spiteful; just change the topics in your life that you let them speak into your microphone about. You are in charge, and you have the power to turn down their volume whenever you want.

"Believe you can go from underestimated to unstoppable."

> Make a joyful noise unto the
> LORD, all ye lands.
> Serve the LORD with gladness: Come
> before his presence with singing.
> Know ye that the LORD he is God:
> It is he that hath made us,
> and not we ourselves;
> We are his people, and the
> sheep of his pasture.
> Enter into his gates with thanksgiving,
> And into his courts with praise:
> Be thankful unto him, and bless his name.
> For the LORD is good; his mercy is everlasting;
> And his truth endureth to all generations.

Psalm 100

Dear Lord

Thank you for being the omnipotent God in my life. I joyously accept your will for the next chapter.

Please fill my heart with humility and grateful acceptance. Open the doors you want me to walk through as I continue down my career path. Equip me with the skills, knowledge, and wisdom to stay ahead of the process.

Thank you for being my best friend all along. I trust you and want more of you every day.

For the CPS (CADJPro Payroll Solutions) crew with me on this "plane," bless them to take off with me and fill the air beneath our wings with encouragement and instruction.

Offload any unnecessary baggage before we get to our next stop so those opposed to our success cannot hinder us on your path.

You are the God of Sacrifice, the omnipresent God, and my work will live in the purpose you designed just for me. Thank you for what is ordained ahead of me by your Grace.

Bless the reader with strength and determination to succeed on their journey.

In Your Name,

Amen

Manufactured by Amazon.ca
Bolton, ON